PROTEIN FOODS
Are Good for You!

by
Gloria Koster

PEBBLE
a capstone imprint

Published by Pebble, an imprint of Capstone
1710 Roe Crest Drive
North Mankato, Minnesota 56003
capstonepub.com

Library of Congress Cataloging-in-Publication Data is available on the Library of Congress website.

ISBN: 9781666351279 (hardcover)
ISBN: 9781666351330 (paperback)
ISBN: 9781666351392 (ebook PDF)

Summary: Almonds, eggs, and beans . . . . What do these protein foods have in common? They're all healthy! Discover where protein foods come from, what nutrition they provide, and how they help form a healthy diet. Filled with meaty facts, including meat alternatives, this Pebble Explore book will give curious young readers plenty to chew on.

Editorial Credits
Editor: Donald Lemke; Designer: Tracy Davies; Media Researcher: Julie De Adder; Production Specialist: Katy LaVigne

Image Credits
Getty Images: Andrew Olney, 6, chanyanut ganpanjanee, 17, FatCamera, 29, JimmyFam, 28, Jose Luis Pelaez Inc, 5, Jupiterimages, 14, Makidotvn, 25, marcduf, 9, PacoRomero, 18, The Good Brigade, 23, vaaseenaa, 20, Westend61, 15; Shutterstock: Africa Studio, 26, Arina P Habich, 4, DenisNata, cover (front), Designua, 12, hudhud94 (beef steak doodle), cover, 3, Ildi Papp, 21, inewsfoto, 24, Iraida Bearlala (background), cover and throughout, JenJ_Payless, 13, margouillat photo, 8, Monkey Business Images, 16, Oliver Hoffmann, 7, Prostock-studio, 19, 22, Tatyana Aksenova, 27, Vasilinka (doodles), cover and throughout, wasapohn (nuts doodles), cover, 1, 3; USDA: 11

All internet sites appearing in back matter were available and accurate when this book was sent to press.

Printed and bound in the USA.   4882

TABLE OF CONTENTS

Words in **bold** are defined in the glossary.

PROTEIN PACKED

Welcome to a summer cookout!
People grill turkey burgers and chicken.
Someone brings a bean salad to share.
Others dip vegetables into hummus.

This cookout is packed with protein!

Meat has a lot of protein. Veggies have protein too. Many are healthy foods. They build muscles and keep our hair, bones, and **organs** healthy.

Think of all the protein foods. Do you like fish sticks? Protein is in fish and seafood. What about eggs? Scramble some for a healthy breakfast.

Other protein foods come from plants. Beans and peas are plant proteins. Nuts and seeds are too.

Beans, peas, and nuts are protein foods.

salmon

Choosing healthy protein foods is important. Fried chicken and hamburgers can taste good. These foods also have a lot of fat.

Choose meats with less fat and salt. Chicken breasts can be a good choice. Some fish, like salmon, is a healthy choice too.

Hot dogs, lunch meats, and sausages have protein. But these foods often have a lot of salt. Don't eat them too often.

MyPlate is a guide for healthy meals. Half your plate should have fruits and vegetables. Half should have grains and protein foods. A small amount of **dairy** is on the side.

Why are these foods good for you? They have **nutrients**. Nutrients keep you healthy. They help your body grow. Protein is a nutrient.

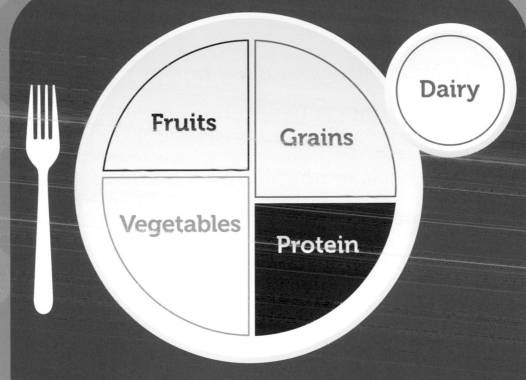

MyPlate.gov

PROTEIN AND YOUR BODY

Every cell in your body has protein. But how does it get there?

Protein is made of **amino acids**. Your body already makes some amino acids. Others come from food.

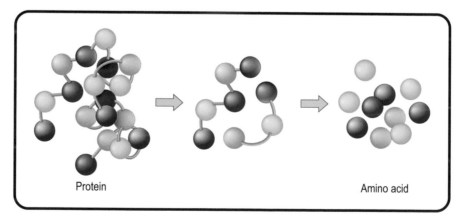

Protein

Amino acid

Proteins become amino acids in your stomach.

Amino acids break down when you eat. They travel around your body. They carry **oxygen**. They deliver vitamins and minerals.

Protein does many jobs. It builds strong muscles and bones. It makes new skin and hair. Protein heals cuts. It helps keep you from getting sick.

What if you don't get enough
protein? You may feel tired. Cuts may
take a long time to heal. You may have
aches and pains.

How much protein do you need?

Not everyone needs the same amount of protein. The amount depends on your age and size. It depends on how much you move. But most kids need about two servings a day.

Protein foods are important for good health. But you don't need to eat all your protein at once. Your body cannot store extra protein.

PLANT PROTEIN

Some people are **vegetarians**. They do not eat meat, like beef, chicken, or fish. They get protein from other foods.

Spinach and milk have a lot of protein.

Some people are **vegans**. Like
vegetarians, they do not eat meat.
They don't eat any products that come
from animals. Dairy and eggs are
types of animal products.

Animal protein has all the amino acids you need. Most plants do not. You may need to eat several plant foods together for enough protein.

tofu with other plant foods

quinoa salad

Soybeans are high in protein. Tofu is made from soybeans. **Quinoa** has as much protein as meat. Quinoa is called a "superfood" because it is so healthy.

PROTEIN POWER

Go grocery shopping with a grown-up. Look at the food labels and food packages. Find foods with healthy proteins.

Then be a helper in the kitchen!
Do you like tacos? Fill them with your
favorite meats and veggies. Cook a pot
of chili with many different beans. Or
grill **kabobs** full of protein foods.

nut butter with apple slices

Protein foods are great snacks! Your body **digests** protein slowly. You stay full longer. You might avoid junk food.

Dip celery sticks into hummus. Spread nut butter on apple slices. Grab a handful of sunflower seeds.

Have some cheese or yogurt. These are types of dairy foods. They also have a lot protein.

Do you play sports? Then you might have tried protein bars. These make quick and easy snacks. They give you a boost of protein. Just make sure they don't have too much sugar.

Remember, some people cannot eat certain foods. They may be **allergic** to eggs or nuts. They may have a **gluten** allergy. Gluten is a protein in wheat and other grains.

People with allergies often find other foods they like. Some use almond butter instead of peanut butter. Others use chickpea water instead of eggs.

chickpea water

Try to get enough protein every day. Remember to get lots of exercise too! Go for a bike ride. Play your favorite sport with friends. Try yoga!

These activities and protein foods
will help keep you healthy and strong
for years to come.

GLOSSARY

allergic (uh-LUR-jik)—unpleasant reactions, like sneezing or a rash, to certain foods

amino acid (UH-mee-noh AA-sid)—any of many acids that occur naturally in living things and that include some that form proteins

dairy (DAIR-ee)—products made with milk

digest (dye-JEST)—the process of breaking down foods in the stomach and organs, so it can be used in the body

gluten (GLOO-tuhn)—a part of wheat and flour that holds dough together

kabobs (kuh-BOBZ)—small pieces of meat or vegetables cooked on a skewer

nutrients (NOO-tree-uhnts)—the parts of food that are needed for growth and health

organs (OR-guhnz)—a part of the body that does a particular job; the heart, liver, and lungs are organs

oxygen (OK-suh-juhn)—a colorless gas that humans and animals use to breathe

quinoa (KEEN-wah)—starchy seeds which are used as food and ground into flour

vegan (VEE-gehn)—a person who does not eat food or use products that come from animals

vegetarian (vej-uh-TER-ee-uhn)—a person who does not eat meat

READ MORE

Schuh, Mari. *Food Is Fuel*. Mankato, MN: Capstone, 2020.

Schwartz, Heather E. *Cookie Monster's Foodie Truck: A Sesame Street Celebration of Food*. Minneapolis: Lerner Publications, 2020.

Webster, Christy. *Follow that Food!* New York: Random House, 2021.

INTERNET SITES

USDA MyPlate: "Protein Foods"
myplate.gov/eat-healthy/protein-foods

Harvard School of Public Health: "The Nutrition Source"
hsph.harvard.edu/nutritionsource/what-should-you-eat/protein

Healthy Kids Association: "Meat, Poultry, Fish, Eggs and More"
healthy-kids.com.au/food-nutrition/5-food-groups/meat-alternatives

Verywell Family: "Protein-Rich Foods for Kids"
verywellfamily.com/protein-rich-foods-2633936

INDEX

ABOUT THE AUTHOR

A public and school librarian, Gloria Koster belongs to the Children's Book Committee of Bank Street College of Education. She enjoys both city and country life, dividing her time between Manhattan and the small town of Pound Ridge, New York. Gloria has three adult children and a bunch of energetic grandkids.